BANGLADESH
RIVERS IN A CROWDED LAND

by Vimala McClure

DILLON PRESS, INC.
Minneapolis, Minnesota 55415

Acknowledgments

The author wishes to warmly thank the following people: Ms. Kathy Runde, Ms. Yasmin Rahman, Ms. Zeenat Khan, Ms. Sartaz Aziz, Ms. Rina Sen, Mr. S. A. Reza Hussain, Mr. S. M. Tariq Khan, Mr. S. Roy of the Uddayan Bidyalaya School, Mr. Tapan Banerjee, Mr. Aftabuddin Ahmad of Bangladesh Biman, and Dr. Shah Jahan Mohd of the Bangladesh Association.

Special thanks to the Bangladesh Parjatan Corporation, and in particular to Mr. Bijon Sarkar, staff photographer, for graciously supplying many of the photographs in this book. Other photographs are reproduced through the courtesy of the Bangladesh Association of New England, the Embassy of Bangladesh, Vimala McClure, UPI/Bettman Newsphotos, and World Vision (Bruce Brander and F. D. Haidar, photographers).

Library of Congress Cataloging-in-Publication Data

McClure, Vimala Schneider, 1952-
    Bangladesh : rivers in a crowded land / Vimala McClure.
      p.   cm. — (Discovering our heritage)
    Bibliography: p.
    Includes index.
    Summary: Describes the history, people, folklore, family life, food, schools, and sports of Bangladesh, as well as its immigrants to the United States.
    ISBN 0-87518-404-9
    1. Bangladesh—Juvenile literature. [1. Bangladesh.] I. Title.
II. Series.

DS393.4.M39   1989
954.9'2—dc19   88-35911
                                             CIP
                                           AC

Dillon Press, Inc., 242 Portland Avenue South
Minneapolis, Minnesota 55415

Printed in the United States of America
1 2 3 4 5 6 7 8 9 10 98 97 96 95 94 93 92 91 90 89

Contents

Fast Facts about Bangladesh

Official Name: People's Republic of Bangladesh.

Capital: Dhaka (sometimes spelled Dacca).

Location: Northeastern corner of the South Asian sub-continent. Most of Bangladesh borders on India, except a small part in the extreme southeastern corner, which borders on Burma. The Bay of Bengal forms Bangladesh's southern border.

Area: 55,598 square miles (143,998 square kilometers). *Greatest distances:* north-south—464 miles (747 kilometers); east-west—288 miles (463 kilometers). *Coastline*—357 miles (575 kilometers).

Elevation: *Highest*—4,034 feet (1,230 meters) at Burma border. *Lowest*—sea level.

Population: 109,471,000 (1988 estimate).

Form of Government: Republic. *Head of Government*—president.

Important Products: Jute, rice, tea, wheat, sugarcane, tobacco.

Manufacturing: Jute products, textiles.

Basic Unit of Money: Taka.

Major Language: Bengali.

Major Religions: 83 percent Muslim, 16 percent Hindu, 1 percent Buddhist and Christian.

Flag: A large red circle on a green field. The green represents the scenic beauty of Bangladesh; the red circle represents the rising sun of independence.

National Anthem: "Amar Sonar Bangla" ("My Golden Bengal").

Major Holidays: Id-ul-Fitr (following the Muslim month of Ramadan); Id-ul-Azha (date varies according to the Muslim calendar); Ashura (date varies according to the Muslim calendar); Durga Puja (September through October); Diwali (October); Holi (March or April); Baishakhi Purnima (May); Independence Day (March 26); Bengali New Year's Day (April or May); Victory Day (December 16).

CHINA

BHUTAN

NEPAL

BANGLADESH

NORTH AMERICA

EUROPE

ASIA

AFRICA

SOUTH AMERICA

AUSTRALIA

Saidpur

Jamuna

Mymensingh

Sylhet

Rajshahi

Padma (Ganges)

Meghna

INDIA

Dhaka

BANGLADESH

CHITTAGONG HILLS

INDIA

Khulna

Noakhali

Chittagong

SUNDARBANS

MOUTHS OF THE PADMA (GANGES)

Cox's Bazar

BURMA

Bay of Bengal

N

1. A Land of Water and People

Until 1971, no one had ever heard of Bangladesh, the lush land once known as East Bengal and East Pakistan. Yet this land of green rice paddies and rushing rivers, of scorching sun and raging storms, has existed for thousands of years. Not until 1971, though, did Bangladesh become an independent nation. For many centuries before that, it was part of India, and more recently Pakistan.

The people of Bangladesh, called Bangladeshis, share a common heritage with the people of the neighboring land of West Bengal, a state in the country of India. In fact, the name *Bangladesh* means *Bengal nation*, and more than 95 percent of all Bangladeshis are Bengalis, a generally short, dark-skinned people who also live in West Bengal. They speak a language called Bengali, which is the official language of Bangladesh.

Bangladesh is a small country in the northeastern corner of the South Asian subcontinent. It is surrounded by India except along the extreme southeastern part, which borders Burma, and along the southern coast on the Bay of Bengal. Many small islands near the coast are also part of the nation.

Rivers in a Crowded Land

Water and people are the two most striking features of Bangladesh. More than 100 million people crowd into a nation the size of Wisconsin. For the United States to be that crowded, all the people in the entire world would have to live within its borders!

Over much of this South Asian nation, the land is sandy, clay soil deposited by three big rivers and the many streams that flow out from them. These rivers are very important in both India and Bangladesh because they provide fertile farmland for crops and water for the needs of millions of people.

The largest mountains in the world, the towering Himalayas, are located just north of Bangladesh. High in the Himalayas, the Ganges River begins. It gathers water in Nepal and India and then enters Bangladesh, where its name changes to Padma. The Brahmaputra River also has its source in the Himalayas. It flows through Tibet and the Indian state of Assam before entering Bangladesh, where it is called the Jamuna and joins with the Padma. The third river, called the Meghna, rises in the hills of Bangladesh near the town of Sylhet in the north, and joins with the others to flow down into the Indian Ocean at the Bay of Bengal. Bangladesh's coastline is one huge river delta, the largest in the world.

This woman and her daughter are only two of more than 100 million Bangladeshis.

Boats transporting goods are a common sight on Bangladesh's many waterways.

Waterways, Farms, and Floods

The river systems provide a valuable means of transportation throughout Bangladesh. Along the nation's more than 2,500 waterways, ships and boats of all sizes carry goods and people back and forth across the land. During the rainy season, simple hand-powered boats are sometimes the only way to visit neighbors or to travel into the cities from the villages.

For most of the year, the weather is hot and humid. Starting in June, the clouds gather, and rain falls in heavy downpours during the three-to-four-month monsoon season. The rivers flood, and the country becomes a vast muddy lake with brilliant green rice fields rising from the water like large square emeralds. Sometimes the weather can be fierce. Cyclones roar through the Bay of Bengal and actually make the rivers flow backward, with winds of 100 miles (161 kilometers) per hour and waves up to thirty feet (nine meters) high. A cyclone and tidal wave caused the country's greatest natural disaster in 1970, when about 266,000 people were killed by the huge waves and raging floodwaters.

Because Bangladesh has so many people, some have moved to the coastal areas to find land where they can farm and raise their families. In these areas, storms can destroy entire villages in a single day. When a cyclone struck the coastal islands in May 1986, 10,000 people and a half-million head of cattle were killed in thirty-six hours. Most of the homes in the area were destroyed, and an entire island with all of its inhabitants was swept away.

The climate and the rivers provide just the right soil for Bangladesh's crops: jute, rice, sugarcane, and tea. Jute, which means "matted hair," is the nation's main cash crop. Fibers from the jute plant are made into twine, rope, burlap, and other textiles and exported to

many countries around the world. Rice forms an essential part of the Bengali diet, so it too is a very important crop.

Khulna Division

Bangladesh is divided into four regional areas, called divisions. Each division is separate in some ways, like a state in the United States, and each has its special characteristics. The Khulna Division in the south, which borders the Indian state of West Bengal, is made up of swampy marshland much like that of the Louisiana delta in the United States. The city of Khulna is the third largest in the country; some of the biggest factories and mills are located there.

The Sundarbans, a huge wildlife sanctuary, is located in the Khulna Division. It is a dense forest with thousands of streams, some of which flow backward when the incoming ocean tide is stronger than the rivers that flow down from the mountains. Crocodiles and huge pythons hunt the streams and rivers, and the trees are full of the songs of tropical birds. The Sundarbans is also home to magnificent tigers, monkeys, elephants, bears, and beautiful spotted deer.

The majestic Bengal tigers roam throughout this wildlife sanctuary. They live for about sixteen years and grow to about thirteen feet (four meters) in length. At

Floods often cause great damage in Bangladesh. In 1988, flooding turned the streets of the capital city into a lake.

one time it was feared that the tigers would completely disappear because of hunting. Since tiger hunting was banned in the 1970s, though, they have begun to reclaim their place as kings of the jungle in Bangladesh.

In the wintertime, a festival is held on a small island in the Sundarbans. Hundreds of fishermen come from all over the district to participate in days of buying, selling, fishing, and making friends. Gypsy families who live on houseboats in the area use trained otters to catch fish. They put a net at the bottom of a stream and release the otters upstream; the otters quickly chase the fish into the net.

Dhaka

Dhaka Division is in the center of the country, crisscrossed by the three great rivers—the Jamuna, the Padma, and the Meghna. More than two million people live in Dhaka, the capital and largest city. Bangladesh is a republic, governed by a president, a cabinet, and a parliament. The newly completed National Parliament Building in Dhaka houses the 330 members who make the nation's laws. Three hundred members are elected by the people; the other thirty seats are specially reserved for women.

Dhaka has a large university, factories, and many big businesses. Huge new apartment buildings and

Elephants live in the Sundarbans and are sometimes trained as work animals.

The skyline of Dhaka, Bangladesh's capital and largest city.

luxury hotels stand alongside sprawling slums where a family of ten might live in a one-room, mud-floored hut. Like other big cities, Dhaka has movie theaters, museums, and a sports arena. On weekday evenings, thousands of soccer fans travel to Dhaka Stadium to watch their favorite teams play.

Only the wealthy have cars in Dhaka. Most people get around by walking, by riding bicycles, or by taking bicycle rickshaws. The bicycle rickshaws provide jobs for many teenage boys who work long hours for the little money that may support an entire family. The

A bicycle rickshaw in Dhaka.

rickshaws are gaily decorated in bright colors, with tinsel and streamers hanging from the awnings and handlebars. Another form of transportation is the auto rickshaw—often called a "baby taxi"—a motor scooter with a covered platform for two to four passengers.

Food and other items are sold in colorful open-air markets in Old Dhaka, the part of the city where little modern development has taken place. Stalls on street corners sell fresh sweets or deep-fried snacks such as *shingaras*—spicy meat- or vegetable-filled pastries.

Rajshahi and Chittagong

Rajshahi Division is in the northwest, where the Ganges River enters Bangladesh. At this point, the mighty river is almost twelve miles (nineteen kilometers) across. There are many ancient ruins in Rajshahi Division, including a huge Buddhist monastery, Hindu temples, Muslim mosques, and palaces built centuries ago. Sugarcane and silk are important products.

Chittagong Division borders the Indian states of Assam and Tripura, and the nation of Burma in the south. Chittagong is the second largest city in Bangladesh. It has the country's busiest port and the only steel mill and oil refinery.

This part of Bangladesh attracts many visitors because of its beautiful hilly areas and beaches. Near

Many ancient Muslim mosques, such as this one, are still in use in Bangladesh today.

the town of Cox's Bazar is the longest shark-free swimming beach in the world, along the silver-blue waters of the Bay of Bengal. Tropical forests cover the Chittagong Hills, a region where many of Bangladesh's native tribes live. Tea is grown on the hills of Sylhet to the north.

Villages and Families

About four of every five Bangladeshis live in villages and make their living by farming the rich soil

A view of the city of Chittagong from the nearby hills.

formed by the rivers and streams. A village may have from 500 to 1,500 people in large extended families. Children, parents, aunts, uncles, cousins, and grandparents all live together. A typical village house is made of mud bricks with a thatched roof. It has one or two rooms and an outdoor courtyard, which is used as a "living room." Since most villages have no electricity or plumbing, water for bathing and drinking is taken from wells. Sometimes a family has its own well, but more often the village well is shared by many families. While the men and boys plough the fields, the women and girls carry the laundry to a river or stream and wash it by pounding it upon big slabs of stone.

At home, everyone must help do the work that keeps the family going from day to day. Planting and harvesting, tending livestock, carrying water, and preparing food are all big jobs which require every family member to do his or her share.

An Ancient Heritage

Whether they live in villages or cities, Bangladeshis take pride in their language and culture. Many of the customs, the stories, and the songs and dances of Bangladesh are thousands of years old. In ancient times, stories were written or told in Sanskrit, one of the great classical languages of world history. Several of India's languages came from Sanskrit, including the Bengali language spoken by the Bengalis of Bangladesh.

Though most of the people are very poor and must struggle to meet their daily needs, Bangladeshis love their country. They are proud of both their ancient heritage and their newfound independence.

2. Ancient Traditions in a Young Country

Culture is a combination of the arts, language, and everyday ways of people in a particular place. Bangladeshi culture combines the ancient Bengali culture of northern India and the religious influences of Islam, Hinduism, and Buddhism.

The tribal culture of Bangladesh is represented in the Chittagong Hills and other hilly areas and includes more than thirty tribes with about one million people. Some of these tribes were originally nomads from Burma or from eastern India. Many practice the Buddhist religion but have also been influenced by Hinduism. Their houses are grass huts, and they make their living by farming and by making and selling handicrafts. Some of these tribes have never seen an automobile or heard of electricity or other modern ways of life.

Most Bangladeshis are Bengalis and reflect a mixture of ancient races of dark-skinned Dravidians, light-skinned Aryans, Asian Tibetans, and Burmese. Over hundreds of years, immigrants and invaders from India, Afghanistan, Persia (Iran), Iraq, and Saudi Arabia have settled in Bangladesh. Because of this history, the nation's people are of many different backgrounds with different skin colors and facial structures.

A girl from one of Bangladesh's native tribes stands in a tea field.

Love for Poetry and Art

The Bengali language, music, and literature form important parts of Bangladeshi culture. The language is poetic and expresses many word pictures. For example, the word for mushroom *(vyamer chata)* means "frog's umbrella," and gardenia *(gandharaj)* means "king of scent." Some English words may have originally come from Bengali, such as "veranda" and "pajamas."

The music and literature of the Bengali people are well known in many parts of the world. Bengalis are also known for their love of poetry and politics. Two Bengali poets beloved in Bangladesh are Rabindranath Tagore and Kazi Nazrul Islam.

Rabindranath Tagore is considered one of the world's great poets. He was born in 1861 and died in 1941. Tagore lived much of his life in the part of India that later became Bangladesh. He wrote many beautiful poems, stories, and songs in the Bengali language, including the country's national anthem, *"Amar Sonar Bangla"* ("My Golden Bengal"). Tagore pioneered a new direction in Bengali literature because he wrote in a style that used everyday language instead of the formal language used by poets of the time.

Tagore's new ideas caused many discussions in his day. His stories were the first to show friendships between men and women working together. His women characters came out of the kitchen to argue and exchange ideas with men. Tagore also wrote about the lives of village people. In his stories, the land and rivers are often as important as the human characters.

Tagore was deeply inspired by the beauty of Bengal. He wrote about his childhood in a book called *My Boyhood Days*. He also wrote about the beauty of the Bengali rivers and countryside in many letters to friends all over the world. When the great Irish poet William

Butler Yeats read Tagore's poems, he was very impressed and introduced Tagore's work to the English-speaking world. Tagore was awarded the Nobel Prize for literature in 1913.

Kazi Nazrul Islam—also called Nazrul—lived from 1899 until 1976. He was known as the "rebel poet" because many of his more than three thousand poems were about revolution. His poems helped inspire millions of Muslims to rise against the British government that ruled in what is now India and Bangladesh before 1947. Nazrul once said, "God speaks in the voice of a poet." Much of Bengali poetry—which is often put to music—expresses deeply religious and patriotic feelings and inspires the people to high ideals.

Sculpture and painting are also important in Bengali culture. Hundreds of years ago, artwork was more concerned with religious ideas than it is today. Then, artists were trained in special schools from a very young age. Modern Bangladeshi artists paint traditional scenes as well as beautifully colored designs. Some artists express a concern for others through their art. One famous artist is Masuma Khan. Her paintings are often about the hunger of poor people, the loneliness of young widows, or the suffering of people in war. The artist Zainul Abedin started this tradition. He became famous across the world for his sketches of a famine in Bengal in 1943.

The Art of the People

Because Bangladesh is a land of villages, its finest art is the art of the people—folk art. In the villages, the women gather during the day to rest, talk, and sew the *kantha*, the Bangladeshi patchwork quilt. It is made of bits of worn-out clothing, pieced together and embroidered with thread pulled from the edges. Some kanthas portray village scenes or religious stories. Because nothing goes to waste in a village household, scraps of cloth which cannot be used in a kantha may be used to patch a crack in a wall or pulled apart for thread.

Other useful items are also works of art. Prayer mats made out of reeds by the people of Noakhali have geometric designs woven throughout. The *sika*—a long braid of jute knotted artistically and decorated—is used to hang storage pots from the ceiling. There are carved wooden toys and hand-crafted molds for candy.

Village festivals give Bangladeshis a chance to enjoy traditional music, dance, poetry, and drama. The *jatra*, or folk opera, combines all of these. Jatra is usually performed in a *pandal*, a big, gaily decorated tent. The actors present folk stories, stories about imaginary heroes, and stories from the Hindu and Muslim religions, all accompanied by music and dance.

Bangladeshi children learn traditional folk dances from an early age, usually as part of their playtime

A kantha. *The design is made from individual pieces of cloth.*

activities. Classical music and dances are more complicated, however, and require years of study and practice to master. Many children take lessons in *Manipuri*, a type of dance called the "classical ballet" of Bangladesh. Other children learn to play musical instruments such as the *sitar*, a stringed instrument, or the *tabla* drums.

Muslin, Silk, and Silver

At one time, weavers in Bengal were famous throughout the world for their silks and cottons. The most admired was a fine cotton cloth called *mul-mul*, which is known today as muslin. Bengal's textile industry was one of the greatest in the world, but it was taken over by the British at the end of the seventeenth century. Because the British built large factories, they could produce more cloth at a cheaper price than the Bengalis could. The Bengali weavers were forced to leave their trade, and the variety of cotton plant adapted to the humid Bengali climate gradually became extinct.

As early as 2,000 years ago, muslin was traded for valuable goods in the great city of Sonargaon (pronounced SHON·ar·gow). The ruins of this ancient capital stand outside Dhaka, where they have been restored. Here the government has established the Bangladesh Folk Art Museum, which has many beautiful examples of quilts, utensils, toys, and religious articles. Inside a glass case in the museum is a piece of turban cloth made of Bengali muslin. It is thirty feet (nine meters) in length and three feet (one meter) in width, yet it is so fine that it can be folded to fit inside a matchbox!

Today Bangladesh's famous *jamdani* silks are worn proudly by Bengalis all over the world. These delicate, sheer silks frequently have geometric patterns woven into the cloth, sometimes in gold thread.

Girls in Bangladesh wear dresses or *salwar-kamiz*, an outfit with loose-fitting pants that are tight at the ankle, a tunic that goes below the knees, and a scarf. An

Bangladeshi girls may wear traditional salwar-kamiz *or Western-style dresses.*

older woman might wear a *sari*, a piece of fabric that is six yards (5.5 meters) in length and is wound around the body to make a dress. Boys usually wear T-shirts and shorts or *lungi*s, a colored cloth that is tied around the waist and falls to the ankle. Hindu men in the villages wear *dhotis*—long pieces of white cotton, folded to make loose-fitting trousers. Muslim men wear pants or lungis.

The hill tribes make beautiful silver jewelry. They began to collect silver in the days of British rule by trading for Indian and French coins from Southeast Asia. Heavy necklaces, which look like rings of solid silver, are worn by people in several hill tribes. These necklaces are worn all the time, especially when the person is sick, because the hill people believe that silver binds the soul to the body.

Respect and Good Manners

Most Bangladeshis feel a strong sense of duty toward their families and guests, and will do their best to live up to their social obligations. When visitors come to their home, Bangladeshis will sit and visit with them, and serve them tea and cookies or a meal. Even the poorest families offer all they have to a visitor.

Good manners are important in Bangladesh. People eat with the fingers of their right hand, and a bowl of fresh water is provided for cleaning fingers after the meal. The mother of the household waits until everyone is finished before she eats so she can serve extra helpings and water to her guests. A well-mannered person washes his or her mouth out after eating, and removes his or her shoes before entering the house. It is an insult in Bangladesh to sit with feet pointed at someone else!

A "sweet expression" is the most admirable personal quality that a Bangladeshi can have. A person who must scold someone else will apologize first and use the kindest words and gestures possible. Even strangers address each other as "brother," "sister," "respected mother," and so on.

Bangladeshis generally feel responsible for their family and friends, and try to take care of them. Children are taught from an early age to respect adults, especially their parents. It is rare for a young person to make a major decision alone—parents and older relatives are always consulted.

The Treasures of the Family

In Bangladesh, a baby is given both a "home" name at birth and a "good" name when he or she is a little older. "Home" names are like nicknames. Boys might be called Pappu or Bhola, and girls might be Tinku or Tukul. "Good" names usually reflect the child's heritage and religion. The boy's names Imram and Abdul, and the girl's names Farida and Yasmin are Muslim names. Dilip and Gopal are names for Hindu boys, while Gita and Usha are Hindu girl's names. Often it is hard to tell if a Bangladeshi name is Hindu or Muslim, because religious differences are less important to most Bangladeshis than their cultural heritage.

The good name is given in a special ceremony when the baby first eats solid food. In Muslim families, the naming ceremony is called *Akika*. Relatives and friends are invited to this special festival. An animal is sacrificed, and the *moulvi*, or Muslim priest, reads from the holy book, the *Koran*. Prayers called *sura*s are recited, and the baby's good name is announced. The child is then given a special blessing. Afterwards, there is a feast with special foods and merrymaking. The naming ceremony is a joyous occasion when the new child is officially welcomed to the world.

A new baby is cared for by all the women in the household. The new baby is held, carried, massaged, and caressed constantly. The baby's eyes are decorated with black ointment, and little bracelets are put on its wrists. Babies sleep with their mothers for at least the first two years of their lives.

As children grow older, they spend their time "playing house" and observing everything that happens in a busy home. A three- or four-year-old will watch

Young children receive special attention in Bangladeshi families.

intently as her grandmother offers food and flowers
at the *thakur ghar* (family shrine), chanting and saying prayers or bowing low before the family Koran.
Fathers, brothers, and uncles play a larger part in children's lives as they grow older. In the evening, a father
may sit and teach his child the Bengali alphabet or
verses from the Koran.

In Bangladesh, children are the treasures of their
families and of the culture as a whole. Every Bangladeshi child, rich or poor, grows up with pride in the
nation's ancient traditions. Each child may contribute a
new way to turn those traditions into a brighter future
for Bangladesh.

3. *The Long Road to Independence*

Because Bangladesh was once part of India, it shares much of its early history with that country. As long ago as 1000 B.C., the area which is now Bangladesh was called *Banga* after the Bang tribe that lived there. Throughout its history, Bangladesh has been home to many peoples who fled from invasions in the west, and to others who wanted to conquer new territories for Indian kingdoms. Buddhists and Hindus influenced its culture, but it was the Muslims, starting in the twelfth century, who found the greatest following there.

A Culture with Ancient Roots

The earliest civilized society in India had its origins on the fertile plains of the Indus River, where Pakistan is now. As long ago as 2500 B.C., the area was cultivated by farmers, and great cities were built. These people were the first in India to develop an organized government and many aspects of a modern city, such as water and traffic systems. This early society, called the Harappan civilization, lasted almost a thousand years with very little change.

No one really knows what caused the decline of

Harappan society. Some scholars say that perhaps it was destroyed by the Aryans, who invaded the area from the Himalayan mountain passes in the north. But there is also evidence to suggest that the Harappans migrated east and south and that their culture provided the roots for the modern societies in India and Bangladesh.

Women of Harappa wore bracelets on their wrists and ankles, and braided their hair just as women in India and Bangladesh do today. Harappans had the same type of bathrooms and houses as are common in Bangladesh today. Even children's toys, such as a tiny wheeled cart, are exactly the same as those made thousands of years ago!

Tribes of Aryans—a light-skinned, nomadic, warlike people—invaded villages and cities starting about 1600 B.C. Eventually, Aryans became the main group in northern India, taking over from the dark-skinned Dravidians who were living there at the time. The Aryans brought horses, chariots, and tribal ways which were very different from the Harappans. During the next five hundred years, the Aryans developed a culture which has much in common with present-day life in India. Most notably, the Aryan culture produced the Hindu religion and its epic literature, including the *Ramayana* and the *Mahabharata*. These tales of love and heroes are India's version of "knights in shining armor." The

Toy carts, such as this one from the museum in Sonargaon, have been playthings in Bangladesh for thousands of years.

moral and spiritual lessons in these stories form the basis of many beliefs and ideals in Bangladesh as well as in India. The stories are frequently acted out in village theaters, in music, dance, and drama.

The Aryans are also credited with inventing the caste system. In this system, people were divided into different groups according to their jobs. Each caste had very strict rules about how to dress, eat, bathe, and, especially, how to relate to members of another caste.

Men from one caste were forbidden to marry women from different castes. Caste members were also forbidden to seek jobs outside of those done by their group.

Buddhist and Muslim Rulers

Around 1000 B.C., the area where Bangladesh is today was inhabited by many tribes who may have been fleeing the Aryan invasion in northern India. Some of these were the dark-skinned Dravidians, and others were from the Bang tribe. In the fourth century B.C., Bengal (as this area later came to be called) was part of the Mauryan empire. The greatest Mauryan emperor was Ashoka, who ruled from 274 to 232 B.C. Ashoka had been a war-loving king, but after he became a Buddhist he decided to give up war completely. Instead he sent out missionaries to convert people to his religion. Buddhism gradually became the major religion in the area. It remained important until the arrival of Muslim invaders in the twelfth century.

For much of the next one thousand years, the area of Bengal was left out of the mainstream of Indian history, and not much is known about it. At times local kings ruled in the area, and at other times it was part of Indian empires. A great Buddhist empire, called the Pala empire, rose around A.D. 750. Many Bengalis happily became Buddhists because they disagreed with the caste system that was part of the Hinduism of the Indian empires. However, a group of Hindus called the Senas overthrew the Pala rulers and brought back Hinduism in A.D. 1150.

At the end of the twelfth century, Muslim tribes began invading Bengal. Various Muslim leaders ruled in Bengal over the next six centuries. Bengal was an independent state in the fourteenth and fifteenth centuries, but in 1576 it became part of the Mogul empire, a Muslim empire that also ruled in India. Over time, many Bengalis converted to the Muslim religion, often to avoid the caste system, and it became an important force in the region.

British Influence

The Portuguese were the first Europeans to come to Bengal. They established Christian missions and a trading post at Chittagong in 1517. Bengal became an important port area in international trade, the "gateway to the East." Other Europeans followed the Portuguese, including the British, French, and Dutch. The British soon became the major influence, and during the 1600s, they established trading posts throughout Bengal.

In 1757 the British East India Company, a private business, took over Bengal by winning a battle against Sirajuddaula, a local king. The British government assumed control of Bengal from this company in 1858. All together, the British ruled in what is now India, Pakistan, and Bangladesh for 190 years. Under their rule, problems arose between the Hindus and Muslims, who had lived together peacefully for centuries. Because British India was mostly Hindu, the Muslims in Bengal and other places felt like a minority in the government. In 1906, the Muslim League was founded in Dhaka to represent the interests of the Muslims in British India. Eventually, the league began to ask that a separate Muslim nation be created.

In 1947, after more than 30 years of sometimes violent protest, India achieved independence from Britain. At the same time, a new Muslim nation—Pakistan—was created. Most Muslims already lived in two northern areas of British India: in the northeast, where Bangladesh is today, and in the extreme northwest. To create Pakistan, these two areas were separated from India. The northwest area became West Pakistan. Bengal in the northeast was divided in half. West Bengal remained a state in India, and East Bengal, where mostly Muslims lived, was made into East Pakistan.

East Pakistan

There were problems with trying to run a physically divided country like Pakistan, with one thousand miles

(1,610 kilometers) of India separating its two parts. The capital was in West Pakistan, and the West Pakistanis—a light-skinned, Middle-Eastern-looking people who spoke Urdu—made most of the decisions. Yet the dark-skinned, Asian, Bengali-speaking people in East Pakistan outnumbered the West Pakistanis. In addition, East Pakistan contributed most of the country's foreign-exchange earnings from money made by selling jute to other countries. Still, most of the benefits of that income went to West Pakistan.

Within a few months of the creation of the new nation, the Bengalis began to realize their true position in Pakistan. The West Pakistani government leaders declared that the national language of Pakistan would be "Urdu and no other language." The Bengali representatives in the government were even forbidden to speak their own language!

The Bengalis could not accept this decision. They were proud of the rich literary heritage of their language and felt that it was very much a part of their identity. The movement in favor of the Bengali language began with student protests. At a demonstration at Dhaka University in 1952, the Pakistani police opened fire, killing 26 people and wounding 400 others. This incident is now remembered as the first event in the move toward independence for Bangladesh. The Central Shahid Minar monument in Dhaka is dedicated to the memory of those who died in the language riots of 1952.

One of the leaders of the language movement in the late 1960s was Sheik Mujibur Rahman. Mujib was a fiery speaker. He spoke the Bengali of the common people and worked hard to build his political party, called the Awami League Party, from its popular roots. The Pakistani government put Mujib in prison several times, but this only made him more popular. The Bengalis saw him as a hero who cared about them and about preserving their culture.

In December 1970, there was an election in Pakistan, and Mujib won a majority of the popular vote, which meant that he would become the prime minister of Pakistan. Many West Pakistanis were not happy with the results of this election, and they postponed starting the new government. But a movement was already underway, encouraged by Mujib and the Awami League, to create a new "land of Bengalis" in East Pakistan—Bangladesh. On March 22, 1971, a message from Mujib to the people of Bangladesh appeared on the front page of several newspapers. It said, "This struggle of ours is for the complete freedom of the...people in Bangladesh. Our struggle will go on until our rights are secured....We must be ready for any sacrifice in order to achieve our goal....Jai Bangla! [Victory to the Bengalis!]"

The Central Shahid Minar monument in Dhaka, built in memory of protesters who died in the 1952 language riots.

The War for Independence

The West Pakistani leaders did not want Mujib to start a new government or Bangladesh to be independent. They moved to crush the Awami League and terrorize the East Pakistani Bengalis. They began to kill Bengalis in East Pakistan at midnight on March 25, 1971. This terrible time came to be known as the Crackdown.

Troops from West Pakistan were sent to seize control of Dhaka. For two days, soldiers moved through the city, killing Bengali people, bombing the university, and burning houses and market stalls. Tariq Khan was a boy of fifteen at the time of the Crackdown. He remembers that night:

"I went, with other boys in the area, to block the road, knowing the Pakistani Army was coming. We blocked the road with old cars and trash—whatever we could find. A red car came, with two men in the back. We went to talk to the driver, to request them to turn around, not to enter the city. We thought they were just ordinary people. But when I looked inside, I saw a gun across the man's lap. I saw only a flash of light—I jumped away. In that instant, they had killed my two best friends."

Tariq went home in grief and spent the night with his family, hiding from the soldiers. The next day he went into Dhaka, where he saw hundreds of people dead and mass graves full of bodies. Tariq escaped the city and went to join the *Mukti Bahini,* the Bengali Liberation Force. At fifteen, Tariq became a soldier, a freedom fighter for his country. He was one of the lucky ones who survived the war.

While the liberation army was forming, people began to flee from the attacks in Bangladeshi cities to safety across the border in India. All together, nearly 10 million people left their homes. Because it was difficult for India to meet the needs of its own 500 million people, it did not have the resources to care for the refugees. Finally, the Indian government sent its army to aid Bangladesh against West Pakistan. On December 16, 1971, Pakistan surrendered.

Sartaz Aziz is a Bengali Muslim woman, a teacher who, as a young girl, lived through the war. She remembered what it was like on the day the war finally ended. "The war of liberation ended when the Indian troops came," she explained. "I watched excitedly as the Indians landed in the square across from our house, then ran to the roof to wave to them. It was a momentary slip for which I almost paid with my life. The [Pakistani] soldiers in the street behind saw me waving and opened fire at me. I felt the soft wind from a bullet as it passed an inch from my cheek. I ran downstairs, terrified that they would come to our house and kill us....So

Bangladeshis rejoice as Indian soldiers come to their aid during the war of liberation. The soldiers are carrying a portrait of Sheik Mujibur Rahman.

close to death on that day, yet somehow I survived."

Today the symbol of Bangladesh's freedom is at Savar, just outside of Dhaka. There, a memorial sculpture soars into the sky. Every year, patriotic Bangladeshis lay flowers at this memorial to honor the freedom fighters who died during the struggle to free Bangladesh.

A Difficult Beginning

The Pakistani government had arrested Sheik Mujibur Rahman and kept him in prison while the war raged in Bangladesh. He was released after the war, and in January 1972 he returned triumphantly to Bangladesh. He was proclaimed *Banglabandhu* ("friend of the Bengalis") and named prime minister of the new nation.

People who had fled to India to protect their children from the bloody war returned home by the hundreds of thousands, welcoming Mujib with shouts of *"Jai Bangla!"* Many refugees returned to find their homes and villages destroyed and their relatives killed or missing. A difficult life awaited them, but they were proud of their hard-won freedom and ready to build a new society in their brand-new country.

Bangladesh's losses in the war were great. Just before losing the war, the Pakistani army had executed more than one hundred leading Bangladeshi teachers, poets, artists, and doctors. The army had also destroyed much of the country's wealth, including all the money in the Central Bank in Dhaka. The railroads and shipyards were in ruins, and there was no food for the refugees coming back across the Indian border.

But Bangladesh had also been devastated by the forces of nature. In November 1970, only a few months before the war began, a cyclone and tidal wave had ripped through the countryside. This natural disaster killed more than half a million people and destroyed countless villages. More tragedy awaited. Over the next two years there were major floods. Many people were left homeless and starving.

Mujib's government was overwhelmed by these problems, and he was criticized for not being able to manage the economy. The country's food supply was reduced even further because some people were taking advantage of the struggling new government's lack of control. Smugglers and other people kept large amounts of food in storage. Food prices rose quickly; what little food there was became extremely expensive.

During the summer of 1974, a new round of floods covered two-fifths of the Bangladeshi countryside. Starvation and disease threatened to wipe out most of the population. Mujib could not handle his country's huge problems. He tried to control the government, but critics said that he misused the military and allowed crime to go unstopped throughout the country.

In the beginning of 1975, millions of homeless, starving people crowded the streets of Dhaka. Under Mujib's orders, the army police made three camps outside the city and moved more than fifty thousand homeless people there. The camps were surrounded by barbed wire and guarded by the *Rakhi Bahini*, Mujib's hand-picked police. There were no building materials,

A memorial to Sheik Mujibur Rahman marks the spot where he was killed in 1975.

no medical supplies, no means of income, and only tiny rations of food. Many thousands of people died.

The camps were a turning point. People began to blame Mujib for the crisis in the new nation. Dissatisfied military leaders killed him and most of his family in August 1975. The nation was put under martial law—the military took over the government and banned all political meetings. Over the next few months, leadership of the nation changed hands several times.

Two Presidents

In 1976, the head of the army, General Ziaur Rahman, took over as president. President Zia, as he was called, formed the Bangladesh Nationalist Party. He ended martial law and restored a democratic government to Bangladesh. President Zia worked hard to establish good relations with Western and Islamic countries. He visited more than thirty countries in five years and brought many world leaders to Dhaka on return visits. They responded by helping Bangladesh with money, food, and business. President Zia also won Bangladesh a seat on the United Nations Security Council.

However, the problems of the vast majority of Bangladeshi citizens went unsolved, and the gap between the rich military government and the poor farmers in the villages widened. President Zia was losing support, and his government was severely weakened by violence. Many military leaders were not satisfied with the way the government was being run. On May 30, 1981, President Zia was killed by rebelling army officers.

In 1982, General Hossain Mohammed Ershad again put Bangladesh under martial law. Four years later, martial law was lifted, elections were finally held, and President Ershad was re-elected.

In all, the Bangladeshi government was changed or shaken by violence more than twenty times since its

Hossain Mohammed Ershad, president of Bangladesh.

beginning in 1971. However, since 1982, when President Ershad took over, the government has been relatively stable.

The Nation Today

Bangladesh's leaders continue to struggle to maintain a balance between tradition and progress. The gap between rich and poor has not closed, but improvements have been made. Modern technology, including computers and better farming methods, are

being introduced into the country's businesses and farms.

New challenges constantly arise. Recently, a serious conflict in the Chittagong Hills has disturbed the peace and drawn international attention. Many Bengali Muslims have moved to the hill areas to escape the crowded plains, and the tribes who have lived there for thousands of years became afraid that their ancient land and customs would be destroyed by development. They formed the *Shanti Bahini*, an armed group of several thousand guerrilla fighters, to resist the settlement of their lands. In 1986, the government sent troops to patrol the area and closed it off to foreigners and the press. Although recent reports stated that the army has been arresting tribal people without cause and encouraging the Bengali settlers to attack them, the government has denied it. President Ershad said that he wants the hill people to "march with the mainstream and forget about this bitter experience." But many tribal people continue to resist.

The sometimes fierce weather has also continued to cause problems for the Bangladeshi government. In the fall of 1988, unusually heavy floodwaters covered three-fourths of the Bangladeshi countryside, leaving nearly 30 million people homeless or stranded. The country had to rely on the aid of other countries to keep its people from starving.

Many Bangladeshis who in 1971 looked forward

Modern technology, such as this tower for transmitting electricity, can be found alongside traditional ways of life in Bangladesh.

with joy to their country's freedom now feel frustrated by the long, slow process of building a nation which can meet the needs of its citizens. Yet the people's deep love for their culture continues to inspire them to work hard for a more prosperous future.

Flood victims wade through the streets of Dhaka to receive aid during the 1988 disaster.

4. *Tales of Foolish Kings and Tiger Gods*

Every Bangladeshi child grows up hearing stories from grandparents, aunts and uncles, brothers and sisters, parents and teachers. Some are religious stories, some are stories about everyday things, and some have funny twists or endings which teach a lesson. Bangladeshi stories and poetry reflect the land, the weather, and the customs and values of the people. There are many love stories, with strong heroes, evil demons who kidnap innocent maidens, and tragic endings. The stories are often passed on from parent to child for generations.

In Bengali stories, the kings and proud upper-class people are often fooled or outsmarted by the poorest of their subjects. There are thousands of popular folk stories about the Maharaja (great king) Krishnachandra and his wily jester, Gopal Bhar. Here is one funny story that makes a serious point.

One day the Maharaja Krishnachandra called his jester, Gopal. "Gopal, from now on you should show me more respect," said the king. "Do you realize what a vast difference there is between you and me, between your station and mine? You must respect me accordingly."

Gopal jumped up from his seat. He measured from

The maharajas *of ancient Bengal often rode on beautifully deco-rated elephants such as this one.*

the place where he was sitting to the king's throne.

"O king," he replied. "There is not so much difference. It is only three feet!"

The King Who Liked to Be Clean

Another type of story that is common in Bangladesh is the story that explains an everyday fact of life. In the following story, which can be told in several different versions, a foolish king learns a lesson, and everyone benefits.

Once upon a time, long ago in the great land of Bengal, there was a king who liked everything to be very clean. One day upon stepping out of his bath, he noticed that his feet became dirty as soon as they touched the ground.

"Minister!" he bellowed, summoning his faithful servant. "You must solve this problem immediately. I cannot tolerate all this dirt!"

The faithful minister, being ever concerned about his master's welfare (not to mention his own head!), gathered all the great scientists and scholars together to solve the king's problem. They thought and thought, and argued and argued. By the end of the first day, their brains were hot, but no answer came. By the end of the second day, their thinking steamed up the whole palace, but no result was found. By the end of the third day, the heat from their arguments made the whole kingdom miserable. Finally, a solution was agreed upon.

"O great king," proclaimed the faithful minister. "We have found a solution. We will sweep away all the dirt."

So they purchased thirteen million brooms for thirteen million sweepers across the land. The sweepers swept and swept, and a great dust storm rose up over the land. Coughing and wheezing, the king called the minister.

"Fool!" he shouted. "This will not work! I'll give you three days to find another solution."

So again the minister called all the great thinkers in the kingdom. They used up three hundred pounds of snuff and drank up three thousand pots of tea, and finally came to a decision. They would wash away all the dirt!

So ninety million barrels of water were brought and poured out over the ground. The water rose until it covered everything. Even the fishes were drowning. Everybody in the whole country learned to swim, but they all caught terrible colds because their feet were always wet. Even the king coughed and sneezed, and finally he called his faithful minister.

"Idiot!" he squeaked. "Your cures are worse than the disease! Three days more, then zzzt! Off with your head!"

The faithful minister bowed with folded hands, grateful that his head was still in place. Again a meeting was called, and all the great scientists thought and thought, and argued and argued. They thought so hard that the clouds disappeared and all the water dried up. Finally, the ultimate solution was found. They would cover the whole country in leather so that the dirt could not get through it.

So they called all the cobblers and ordered them to stitch a covering for the whole kingdom, from sea to sea. The king was very pleased. He granted degrees to all the scholars and bestowed medals on all the scientists. Everyone was happy except the farmers, who secretly worried that if the dirt couldn't get through, neither could the crops, and everyone would starve. But no one said a word, and the celebrations went on.

The king issued a proclamation praising the wonderful accomplishments of his cabinet. When he was finished, the oldest of the cobblers stepped forward.

"O great king, may I speak?"

"Yes," replied the king. "What is it, old man?"

"Sire, you do not need to cover the whole world with leather."

"What!" the king spluttered. "You, a low-caste cobbler, argue with the greatest scholars in the land?"

Without another word, the cobbler knelt before the king and placed a pair of leather sandals on his feet.

Astonished at the wonderful invention, the king jumped for joy. From that day onward, all the people wore shoes to keep their feet clean and dry.

Kernels of Wisdom

Bangladeshi stories reflect a love of silly, exaggerated situations. They usually contain a kernel of wisdom, which is also true of Bangladeshi proverbs and sayings. A proverb is a saying that tells something wise or true. Proverbs are very popular in Bangladesh. Some are Bengali versions of sayings that are also known in the United States. For example, Americans might say "Mind your own business" to a busybody. The Bengali equivalent is "Oil your own machine."

Other Bengali sayings are unique. To a person who says something silly, a Bangladeshi might say, "What doesn't a goat eat...and what doesn't a crazy person say!" A Bangladeshi would feel insulted if he or she were helping another person and that person questioned the reason for the help. A proverb that might be used in this situation is, "He, for whom I am stealing, is calling me a thief!"

In Bangladesh, fresh cow dung is made into patties and dried in the sun. The sun-baking removes the smell, and the hard, dry dung cakes are then used for fuel. A Bengali proverb often told when someone laughs at another's discomfort is, "While the dry fuel is burning, the fresh dung is laughing."

The Tiger God

All Bangladeshi children, regardless of their religion, grow up hearing stories about the adventures of Hindu gods and goddesses. The tribes of the Sundarbans have a special favorite, the folk-god Dakshin Rai. Some people say that Dakshin Rai was a real person in the early history of Bangladesh. They say that he was a great tribal king in the south who killed ferocious tigers and fought off invaders. Because Dakshin Rai was killed by a tiger, his spirit is restless and takes revenge on any tiger who tries to kill people who worship him. He is often called the Tiger God, and people pray to him for protection against the tigers of the Sundarbans.

At holiday times, grandmothers and grandfathers tell familiar folk stories about gods and saints, kings and cobras. Each story is full of fun and fright and has a lesson to be carried into everyday life. Like children everywhere, Bangladeshi children want to hear their stories again and again. When they grow up, they tell their own children about the wonders of their ancient land.

5. Many Religions, Many Celebrations

Although more than four of every five Bangladeshis are Muslims, there are also many Hindus, Buddhists, and Christians in this small country. Bangladeshi people from different religions often celebrate one another's festivals and holidays. They accept others with different religious beliefs because throughout its history Bangladesh has been home to many religions. In fact, most Bengalis have ancestors whose religious beliefs were different from theirs. Someone who is a Muslim today might have a grandfather who is a Hindu, and a Buddhist great-great-grandfather!

Followers of Islam

Muslims are followers of the Islamic religion. They pray to *Allah*, their name for God, five times a day, and they frequently read their holy book, called the Koran. On Fridays, men worship in temples called *mosques*, while the women stay inside their homes to pray.

Some Muslim women wear a *burkha*—a long veil which covers the woman from her head all the way to the ground, with a screen across the eyes so that she can see out. The burkha is part of a Muslim custom called

A Muslim mosque in Dhaka.

purdah. In this custom, women are not allowed to let any man, except close relatives, see them. This custom is slowly changing. Most Bengali Muslim women do not keep purdah by wearing veils, but they do stay inside their homes most of the time.

Muslim holidays are called *Ids.* The dates for these holidays change each year because the Muslim calendar follows the cycles of the moon, which are shorter than the months on the Western calendar. A Muslim festival

Children pray during the celebration of a Muslim Id.

celebrated on October 20 one year could be celebrated on October 10 the next. It takes thirty-two years for a festival to fall on the same day in the Western calendar again.

The ninth month of the Muslim year is called *Ramadan*. During this month Muslims are required to fast—to go without food or drink—each day from sunrise to sunset. Fasting during the day is followed by feasting at night. Children and sick people are not required to fast. This month of fasting and feasting celebrates an important event from the beginning of Islam, when the Koran, which Muslims believe contains God's own words, was spoken to the Prophet Mohammed by an angel. Mohammed later founded the Islamic religion.

Ramadan is followed by the joyous holiday *Id-ul-Fitr*, the most important festival in Bangladesh. This holiday starts when the first sliver of the new moon appears after Ramadan. Friends call to one another, *"Chand Mubarak!"* ("Happy Moon to you!"). Special services are held in the mosques, and people give food to the poor. Relatives come to visit, the women prepare all the best foods, and everyone exchanges gifts.

Another special Muslim holiday is *Id-ul-Azha*, also called the *Korbani* sacrifice. This holiday happens on the tenth day of the Muslim month of *Zilhaj*. On this day, people remember the story of how Allah tested the prophet Abraham by commanding him to kill his young son. Abraham wanted to show his obedience, and sorrowfully he raised his hand to kill his son. At the last moment, an angel took hold of Abraham's arm and said that Allah did not want his son to die—Abraham had proven his faith. Joyfully, Abraham killed a ram instead, as a sacrifice to Allah. For this reason, on

A procession celebrating the Muslim holiday of Ashura.

Id-ul-Azha people eat special lamb dishes and give food
to the poor.

The holiday *Ashura* occurs in the first ten days of
Maharram, the first month of the Muslim calendar. On
Ashura, people remember the death of the Prophet Mohammed's grandson Hussain, who was killed by his
father's enemies. Crowds of Muslims carry a statue of
Hussain's tomb through the streets, similar to a funeral
procession.

The Mystic Sufis

Sufism is a branch of Islam which teaches self-knowledge and meditation (sitting quietly and thinking about God). The Sufis are known as the "mystic voices of Islam." Sufism started in the eighth century and greatly influences many Bengali Muslims today.

The writings of Abu Hamid al-Ghazzali form an important part of the Sufi tradition. Al-Ghazzali, who lived from A.D. 1058 to 1111, was an excellent student of Islamic religion, a professor, and a religious teacher. There are many stories about al-Ghazzali. Here is one that shows a serious side to his character.

One day during his student years, al-Ghazzali was returning home from school when a band of robbers attacked him and took all his possessions, including his lecture notes. Al-Ghazzali ran after the thieves and begged them to return his notes. The robbers asked him why pieces of paper meant so much to him, and he replied that there was learning in them. The robber leader laughed and returned the notes to him, saying, "Knowledge that can be stolen is no knowledge at all." Al-Ghazzali felt that this incident was a message from God. He spent the next several years memorizing all his books and the notes from his studies.

Al-Ghazzali achieved much fame and success as a respected teacher. But later in his life, he stopped teaching and spent ten years in quiet prayer and writing. In his writing he said that religion should be a practice (something people do) rather than just a belief. He also wrote that men and women should try to develop the good things about themselves rather than trying to be holy. Al-Ghazzali's teachings later spread to Europe, where they influenced the Christian saints Thomas Aquinas and Francis of Assisi.

The Sufis dance to help bring their minds and bodies into harmony, and to allow their souls to experience oneness with God. "Whirling dervishes" are advanced Sufi students who are taught to dance in a particular way—twirling around and around in a circle—as a form of prayer.

When millions of Bengalis became Muslims in the twelfth century, it was partly because of the influence of Sufism. The Bengalis were attracted by the Sufis' independence, their belief in self-knowledge through meditation, and their belief in equality and justice. The Sufi emphasis on truth and beauty also appealed to the Bengalis, as did the Islamic belief in one God.

Hinduism's Many Gods

Hindus do not have a special day of the week to worship. Most Hindu families have a little shrine in their home, where they can worship every day. They

A Bangladeshi Hindu temple.

can also go to temples to pray and hear spiritual songs and stories.

Hindus believe that each person has an *atman*, or soul, which is reborn again and again in different forms according to what that person has done and said in life. If a person has done good deeds, he or she will be reborn in a higher form. When something bad happens for no apparent reason, Hindus say that it may have been caused by events that happened in past lifetimes.

Many Hindus believe that there is only one God who lives in everything in the universe. However, there are 100,000 names for God, according to Hinduism. They believe that God can appear in just as many forms. Hindus choose to worship the form of God which appeals to them or which has traditionally "sponsored" their family or trade. Every person in a family may pray to a different god, but most of them would say that these are all forms of one God.

Of all the forms for God which Hindus worship in Bangladesh, the most important is the "Mother," the goddess. This goddess can be called Uma, the innocent, or Kali, the fearsome, who takes away life as well as gives it. She can be Durga, the protector and slayer of demons, or Laksmi, who bestows good fortune, or Saraswati, the goddess of wisdom and culture. For Hindus, being a mother means more than just giving birth. The idea of "Mother" is loved, respected, and worshiped.

Hinduism is rich in stories about all the gods and goddesses; throughout the year there are also festivals to celebrate them. Several festivals happen in the fall. *Durga Puja* celebrates the goddess Kali and her victory over evil demons. To celebrate the goddess Laksmi, people decorate their homes with twinkling lights. They also light firecrackers and sparklers because light is supposed to attract Laksmi's blessings. Since Laksmi is the goddess of good fortune, many Hindu business owners start their new business year on this day.

Diwali (also known as *Diipavali*) is a festival of lights, a celebration of peace and harmony. Diwali is celebrated on the day of the new moon in October. There is much dancing, singing, and feasting. Houses are decorated with colored lights, and women beautify the doorsteps of their houses with *rangolis*—pictures made from colored powders or flower petals. Statues of gods and goddesses are also made from flowers and painted clay. These statues are set afloat on the rivers, where they will journey to the sea and dissolve.

Another Hindu festival is *Holi*, which occurs in the spring. It is full of good-natured fun and pranks. Holi celebrates the legend of Krishna, a king who lived in India 5,000 years ago. The Hindus believe that Krishna was God in human form. As a boy, Krishna danced and played with other children, and so Holi is celebrated with folk-dancing, singing, and feasting. People spray colored water at each other, and children drop colored water balloons on unsuspecting people in the streets. It's not a good day to wear your best clothes!

"The Enlightened One"

Buddhism is the third major religion in Bangladesh, practiced mostly by the tribal people in the Chittagong Hills. Buddhists follow the teachings of Siddhartha

Guatama, the founder of Buddhism, who was a prince in India nearly 2,500 years ago. Buddhists tell this story about how their religion was born.

When he was growing up, Prince Siddhartha was sheltered from the world by the walls of his father's beautiful palace. One day when he was a young man, his curiosity grew greater than his fear of disobeying his father's command to remain in the palace garden. Accompanied by his teacher, the prince rode through the palace gate and into the narrow streets and dirty alleys of the city. All around him were poverty, disease, and death. He saw a very old man by the wayside and asked his teacher, "What is this?"

"Why, your highness," replied the teacher. "It is an old man! We will all be old someday."

Prince Siddhartha had never seen an old person before and was shocked. He turned his face away, but he saw another man by the side of the road, covered with disease and with flies swarming around his open sores. At the same time, he heard the sound of mourners carrying a dead woman to her funeral.

The young prince begged his teacher to take him back to the palace. He spent the next days and weeks thinking about the suffering and death he had seen. He realized that it didn't matter how much wealth and comfort he had, or even that he was a prince—suffering, disease, and death would come to everyone.

Prince Siddhartha left his father's palace, determined to find the true meaning of life. He wandered through the country for ten years praying and teaching, until finally he was called the Buddha, which means "the Enlightened One."

Buddhists believe that after the body dies the soul is born again into a new body. They also practice a form of meditation that Buddha taught (similar to the meditation of the Sufis). An important Buddhist holiday is *Baishakhi Purnima*, the birthday of Buddha, which is in May. On this day, Buddhists go to temples and listen to the sermons of their "priests," called *bhikhu*s. They also burn candles and incense before a statue of the Buddha.

Holidays for All

Some special holidays are celebrated by everyone in Bangladesh. March 26 is Independence Day—on this day in 1971 the Bangladeshis declared their nation's independence from Pakistan. Independence Day is celebrated with parades and sporting events such as boat races. Victory Day is celebrated on December 16. This is the day when Bangladesh officially became a country, after the war was over in 1971. Victory Day is also a public holiday and is celebrated with parades, speeches, and military displays.

The Supreme Court Building in Dhaka is lit up to celebrate Bangladesh's Independence Day.

Bengali New Year's Day is the first day of the Bengali month of *Baishakh* (during April or May). This day is celebrated with music, dance, poetry, and drama.

Festivals are very important to people of all religions in Bangladesh. During the festival celebrations, families get together to greet the new babies and remember relatives who have died, neighbors get to know each other better, and all Bangladeshis remember their common heritage.

6. Close-Knit Families, Spicy Food

Boys and girls in Bangladesh spend most of their time separated from each other. They may have classes together in school, but the girls sit on one side of the room, and the boys sit on the other. Boys and girls may be friends if they are relatives. If not, friendships are not allowed between boys and girls over the age of ten unless the young people are closely watched by their parents and other adult family members.

Arranged Marriages

How do Bangladeshi people meet and marry if young men and women are not allowed to be friends? Usually, the parents arrange the marriage, which means they choose the person that their son or daughter will marry. In the past, the bride and groom did not know each other at all until they were married. Today, parents usually introduce the young people before the wedding and allow them to get to know each other a little. Sometimes a marriage is arranged between neighbors or friends—the bride and groom may even have been childhood playmates.

Marriage in Bangladesh is based not necessarily on

love but on mutual respect and family duty. Marriages are not supposed to fail, and divorce is very rare. People believe that love will develop over the course of the marriage. Bangladeshis say that there are advantages to this system. The in-laws are more likely to get along, since they choose their children's mates. This is important because families are close-knit and often live together. Young people go into marriage expecting to carry out the duties defined by their society. They do not expect to be "in love," so when they find love in their marriage, it is especially treasured.

In ancient times, weddings were arranged even before the boy and girl reached their teen years. Yet customs are changing, and today marriages are often delayed until the young people are older. These days, the young people's views are usually considered when arranging marriages. If the boy or girl objects strongly, most parents will not force the couple to marry.

Bangladeshi weddings are as elaborate as the bride's family can afford. The bride wears a red sari decorated in gold. She wears all the jewelry she can— bracelets, head ornaments, rings, earrings, and ankle bracelets. Her hair is decorated with flowers, and she wears a veil to cover her face. The groom arrives at the bride's house riding a horse, escorted by male members of his family. He may wear a turban with a fringe of flowers over the front, so that his face cannot be seen.

Bangladeshi girls prepare a bride for her wedding. In Bangladesh, brides wear elaborate outfits, including decorations made of flowers.

The wedding takes place at the bride's home, and the men and women usually celebrate in separate rooms.

After the wedding, the couple usually moves into the home of the groom's parents. When the new couple arrives, they pay their respects to the groom's mother by bowing at her feet. The bride is now a part of her husband's family. She is required to show respect to her in-laws and to learn the ways of the household from her husband's mother.

Village Life

In Bangladesh, lifestyles are very different for the poor, the middle class, and the wealthy. In the villages, almost all of the families are poor farmers whose hard work earns them barely enough money to live each day. Because most of their food must be processed by hand from seed to harvest to meal, food is the major focus of everyone's daily tasks. Money for other things—cloth, shoes, utensils, or medical care—comes from selling vegetables or handicrafts at local markets.

Villagers spend most of their lives in the fields or in the outdoor courtyards of their mud homes. Inside the houses it is dark because window openings must be kept small to keep out heavy rains. Rooms are bare except for some *charpoy*s—beds made of woven rope. Some houses have "bathrooms," which are enclosed areas with big barrels of water and drains leading outside. To take a bath, people dip a pitcher into the water and splash themselves. Most villagers, though, bathe in one of the many nearby rivers.

Women in the villages get up very early to prepare breakfast—perhaps some tea and dry *chappati*s (round, flat pieces of bread). During the day, they bring water from the village well, tend the family's cattle and other livestock, grind grain, sew, and cook. There are no refrigerators or electric stoves. Most of the cooking is

A village girl sells bracelets in a Bangladeshi market. For many families, the sales from such markets provide money for basic needs such as medical care.

Young Bangladeshi boys haul away the chaff that remains after threshing grain. Most village children in Bangladesh must work to help their families survive.

done outdoors over a fire in the mud hearth.

The men work in the fields all day, tending crops of rice, jute, sugarcane, or tea. Many village children work all day, but sometimes they go to school also. Sometimes the school is not even a building—it may be just a blanket under a banyan tree!

By the age of eight or nine, most village children work from five to nine hours a day. They help take care of younger brothers and sisters, make handicrafts such as embroidered cloth, and weave fishing nets. The boys do the fishing, take care of cattle, strip fibers from the jute plants, haul rice after harvesting, and thresh grain. Girls begin work at six or seven years of age—sweeping, tending chickens, and picking chillies (a type of pepper). By age nine or ten, they help with rice processing, gardening, and cooking.

Lunch for a village child is rice with a bit of fried fish or vegetables. In the evening, the women cook while the men come in from work, bathe, and worship at the household shrine. The men may gather together to drink tea and exchange local news. Supper usually consists of rice or chappatis with vegetables fried in spices. In the evening, the women worship and put the children to bed. By around nine o'clock everything is quiet, and the village goes to sleep.

Life in the Cities

Middle- and upper-class families in Bangladeshi cities live very differently from village families. In the cities, families tend to be a little smaller. It is also more common for nuclear families (mother, father, and children) to live in their own apartment—although relatives may live as close as next door or across the street.

City families may have a breakfast of eggs and toast with fruit or yogurt and tea. Sometimes *suji* is served with fried bread. Suji is cream of wheat made with butter, sugar, and spices such as cardamom and cinnamon. Family members come home for a lunch of rice or bread with spicy meat or vegetables. During the hot season, the juice of the green coconut—called *dav*— is served between meals. Its taste is neither sweet nor bitter, and it is very soothing to the stomach.

Middle- and upper-class children go to school and often take lessons outside of school, studying classical Bengali dances or musical instruments such as the tabla or sitar. Mothers stay home to run the household, while fathers work at jobs in business, industry, or the military. Some middle-class women have part-time jobs outside the home as office workers or teachers.

Most upper-class families have servants to help with the household work, including cooking, cleaning, driving, and shopping. Many city families have televisions. They can watch both Bengali programs and imported shows from Europe and the United States.

Bangladeshi Food

Bangladeshis of all classes and ages like to eat hot, spicy food. These dishes take a lot of time and expert management to prepare. The kitchen belongs to the women and is kept spotlessly clean. No one may enter the kitchen without first removing his or her shoes.

In Bangladeshi kitchens, the cook sits on the floor while preparing food. This woman is serving portions of rice.

Food is prepared while squatting or sitting on the floor, and there are special utensils for cooking in this way.

A *boti* is a special kind of knife used to cut vegetables. It is a long, thin piece of wood with a sharp knife blade attached to it, curving upward. The cook sits on the wooden part and faces the knife. She pushes the vegetables against the blade, and the pieces fall into a bowl in front of her. This can be done at amazing speed but it requires a lot of skill. Another special kitchen utensil is the *shiil nora*, a smooth black stone that is used to grind spices.

In Bangladesh, favorite foods include *biryani*, which is rice with spicy chicken, beef, or mutton, and *dal*, which are spicy cooked lentils. There are also various preparations of fried fish, especially the native *hilsa* fish. Sweets are usually made from milk products and sugar.

There are hundreds of ways to prepare Bangladesh's seasonal vegetables. Usually a *masala*—a fried paste made of ground spices—is made first. Mustard oil is heated, and then freshly ground spices such as turmeric, cumin, ginger, and cardamom are added and fried. Garlic, onions, and hot chillies are added next. Finally, the chopped vegetables are added and fried. Various herbs can be added to change the taste—for example, neem leaves would make it taste bitter, and coriander would make it sweet.

Delicious tropical fruits—including mangoes, small, sweet bananas, and litchis—grow everywhere in Bangladesh. Litchis look like bunches of hard nuts, the size of walnuts. To eat them, you crack open the shell and peel it off. Inside is a sweet white fruit with a round black pit.

Jackfruit (also called *bel*) is quite common in

Typical Bangladeshi sweets. In Bangladesh, sweets are often made of milk products and sugar.

Litchis are cracked open, and the white fruit inside is eaten.

Bangladesh. People call this fruit "God's gift to the poor" because it grows abundantly and is very high in protein. The jackfruit has a hard, knobby shell with one whitish seed inside, which is often fried and eaten. The fruit is brown and juicy. Sometimes it is cooked with vegetables and spices, and at other times it is eaten raw.

For snacks, young people enjoy *muri*—crunchy puffed rice fried in spices. Another favorite is *alu bharta* with *luchi*s—mashed potatoes with flat, round fried bread. You take a piece of the luchi, pick up some of the spicy yellow alu bharta with it, and then pop it in your mouth. Here is a recipe for this popular snack.

Alu Bharta

4 large potatoes
1/8 cup mustard oil
1/4 cup diced onion
1/4 teaspoon diced garlic
1/2 cup grated unsweetened coconut
1 small green chilli, finely diced
1/2 teaspoon diced fresh ginger
1/4 teaspoon turmeric
1/2 teaspoon ground cumin
1/2 teaspoon fresh ground cardamom
1/4 cup fresh chopped coriander
1/2 teaspoon salt
1/2 teaspoon sugar

1. Either bake or boil the potatoes, and peel them. The potatoes should still be warm when you make this recipe.
2. Heat the oil in a heavy skillet at a medium heat.
3. Add the onion, garlic, coconut, chilli, and spices (ginger, turmeric, cumin, and carda-mom) to the oil. Fry this mixture. You may

substitute 1/4 teaspoon of a spice called *hing*, or asafoetida, for the onion and garlic.
4. Add this mixture to the cooked potatoes, and mash. At the same time, add in the coriander, salt, and sugar. Makes four servings.

Luchis

2 cups flour
1 teaspoon salt
2 tablespoons melted butter
water
oil

1. Mix the flour, salt, and butter together in a large bowl. Add enough water to the mixture to make an elastic dough.
2. Roll the dough into thin, round, flat pieces.
3. Fry the thin pieces of dough in hot oil in a heavy skillet. Fry for only about a minute, until the luchi puffs up.
4. Serve with the alu bharta. This recipe makes about 10 luchis.

Many Bangladeshi desserts are special milk sweets which take hours to prepare. One sweet that is easier to make is *burfi*—a delicious caramel fudge flavored with fresh cardamom. Here is a recipe for this dessert.

Burfi

1 cup butter
1-1/2 cups sugar
1 cup evaporated milk
2 to 3 cups powdered milk
1/2 cup slivered almonds or pistachios
2 teaspoons fresh ground cardamom
powdered sugar

1. Melt the butter in a large saucepan, and add the sugar.
2. Add the evaporated milk. Stir the mixture and bring it to a gentle boil.
3. Once the mixture has boiled, lower the heat. Continue to stir, adding the powdered milk a little bit at a time.
4. Add the nuts and cardamom.
5. When the mixture is very thick, spoon it onto a large, oiled cookie sheet. Pat the mixture until it is flat.
6. Refrigerate the burfi for two hours (or let it cool for six hours). Cut the burfi into squares, dust it with powdered sugar, and enjoy!

7. *Learning and Helping Others*

Out of every ten people in Bangladesh, only two can read and write. Although the government and volunteer groups are trying to improve people's chances for a better education, village life is still very hard, and most children cannot finish school.

Work or School

A school in a Bangladeshi village might be as simple as a group of children and their teacher seated under a tree. The children might write on slates (small blackboards) to practice their letters, but often even these are not available. Students learn arithmetic by heart and recite memorized poems and other lessons.

Village children go to school whenever they can. In the villages, however, children must work to help their families survive. Sending their children to school requires sacrifices which are frequently impossible for most rural families to make. During certain seasons, the children must work full-time in sowing, transplanting, harvesting, and processing crops. Most families cannot afford the schoolbooks, paper, and pencils—even the clothing—that is considered proper for school.

Village girls take a break from their farm work. Many Bangladeshi parents do not believe it is necessary for girls to go to school.

Unlike these children, many rural Bangladeshi children do not have the opportunity to go to school.

Village girls, in particular, fall behind in education. Often girls are not sent to school because they must babysit the younger children and because their parents believe that an education is not necessary for them. Most Bangladeshis believe that girls are supposed to marry and have children. In addition, the school may be located far away from the village, and girls are not allowed to travel as freely as boys.

Poor nutrition can also hinder the education of village children. Because many Bangladeshi children do not get enough of the right kinds of foods, their bodies and minds don't develop properly. They are more likely to become sick. Girls usually suffer from poor nutrition more often than boys do. Since boys can earn more money for the family, they are often given a larger share of the food that is available.

Until recently, education involved many subjects that village parents felt their children would never need. In 1983, the school curriculum for upper grades was changed to teach more work skills. Now students can learn farming, for example, while they are learning to read and write. The government hopes that this change, along with more schools and more flexible schedules, will help meet the needs of village children.

City Schools

Like village children, young people who live in the poorer sections of Bangladesh's large towns and cities go to school whenever they can. However, poor children often must go to work at an early age to help pay for their family's food and housing. They may have jobs earning very little money as servants, rickshaw pullers, or flower sellers on street corners. Many of these children begin school at age seven, but have to drop out and go to work as early as the third or fourth grade. Poor nutrition is also a problem among poor children in the cities, because it makes them too sick to study.

Poor children, such as these, in Bangladesh's cities usually have to work at an early age to help support their families.

Even if it is sometimes difficult to get, education is important for many Bangladeshis. This can be seen in the special ceremony they have to welcome a child into the life of knowledge. When the child is old enough to learn the letters of the alphabet, the father prepares him or her for this ceremony, which the Muslims call *Hathi Khori*. The moulvi or other religious leader formally introduces the child to each letter of the alphabet—it may be Arabic, Bengali, English, or all three. In front of friends and relatives, the child reads the letters aloud for the first time. The guests praise the child and give him or her gifts of books. The child is made to feel very important and special.

Children from middle- and upper-income families in the cities go to school regularly. Their families can afford to send them to private schools, to buy their uniforms and schoolbooks, and to maintain the household so that the children have time free to study. Children who are lucky enough to go to school value their education and strive for the best grades they can achieve.

Courses of Study

Schoolchildren in Bangladesh typically wear blue and white uniforms. Classes are big, sometimes as many as fifty children per classroom. Children study

Schoolchildren in Bangladesh's cities typically wear blue and white uniforms. Girls sit on one side of the classroom, and boys sit on the other.

Bengali textbooks and use "copy books"—notebooks in which they write their lessons. They are required to pass tests twice a year and to join in competitive school activities. Since "standing first" (getting the best grades) is a great honor, the students study very hard for the exams.

Schools are conducted in "English medium" or "Bengali medium," referring to the main language used in the school. Classes are held six days a week. They begin early in the morning and end by two in the afternoon. Students are given a one-month vacation from mid-May to mid-June, the hottest season of the year.

Typical school subjects are Bengali, English, mathematics, science, and history. By the ninth grade, students are expected to choose a course of study in either the arts or sciences. A young person who wants to be a teacher will choose the arts courses; someone who wants to be a doctor will choose sciences.

After the tenth grade, qualified students graduate from high school and attend a two-year "college," which is similar to high school in the United States. Without this kind of "college" education, it is very difficult for a young person to get a job which pays enough to support a family. Most students in Bangladesh, however, do not even finish the tenth grade. They must work as laborers or servants, or struggle to survive in family businesses.

Of the students who finish "college," the best may go on to spend two to four years at a university to earn a degree. Dhaka University is one of the most famous universities on the whole South Asian subcontinent. Students from all over India, Pakistan, and Bangladesh attend this university because of its fine reputation. Although more than one hundred university professors and writers were killed during the 1971 war, Bangladesh's system of higher education recovered rapidly, and today the nation has many fine colleges, universities, and technical schools.

Curzon Hall, home of the science department at Dhaka University.

A Daring Woman

In recent years, an increasing number of middle- and upper-class women in Bangladesh have begun to attend institutions of higher education. This can be clearly seen on the Dhaka University campus, where many women are faculty members or attend the medical and law schools. One famous graduate of Dhaka University is Captain Yasmin Rahman, Bangladesh's first and only woman to work as a commercial airline pilot. Her degree in architecture also enables her to design houses in her spare time.

Rahman was in college during the 1971 war, and she remembers that time as an ordeal because she was locked indoors for nine months. "Once during that time we could go out," she said, "to go to the college for exams. It was a terrible time, with bombs dropping everywhere. So many people suffered." When the war was over, Rahman was able to finish her degree and pursue her dream—to go to flight school.

In both her university class and her flight school, Rahman was one of only two women. In a country where men dominate the professions and women rarely hold important jobs, it took a lot of hard work and patience for her to get through those early years. Joining Bangladesh Biman, the nation's only commercial airline, was difficult. The idea of a woman piloting a commercial jet was not easily accepted at first. Now Captain Rahman is a proud member of the airline and flies a sophisticated F28 jet on the Dhaka to Chittagong route. Her husband is also a pilot for Bangladesh Biman. In 1981, they became the first husband-wife team to pilot a commercial flight, from Dhaka to Sylhet.

The Rahmans' daughter, Smita, is first in her class and also studies classical dance. Smita is like many members of the first generation of "true" Bangladeshis

Captain Yasmin Rahman, the first woman to work as a commercial airline pilot in Bangladesh.

who were born after the 1971 war. She plans to continue her education so that she can contribute to the welfare of her country.

Women Helping Women

Many of the educated women in Bangladesh are deeply concerned about the effects of their country's war for independence, which left thousands of women physically and emotionally damaged.

Since 1971, several programs have been started to help victims of the war. One of these organizations, Women for Women, is a research group run by women in Dhaka. It is a place where professors, doctors, lawyers, and sociologists work together to study child care, nutrition, and other issues involving women and children. Women for Women and another group, Concerned Women for Family Planning, hosted a meeting in Dhaka in 1985 as part of the United Nations Decade for Women. Women came from all over the South Asian subcontinent and from other countries, including the United States, to discuss how Bangladeshi women and children could be helped toward a better future.

Projects sponsored by groups such as these have been very successful over the years. These projects include handicraft cooperatives to sell embroidered cloth and other crafts, and loans to poor women to start their own businesses. One program, the Women's Entrepreneurship Development Program, was established in 1982. Government funds were combined with aid from the United States to give loans to poor village women, which they could use to start businesses. One woman who made fishing nets was able to double her profits because of the loan program. She also bought a bicycle rickshaw for her unemployed husband, and he is now able to work as well.

Planning for the Future

In a struggling country such as Bangladesh, the government must plan carefully so that positive changes can be made. Although it is important that all citizens go to school and learn to read and write, school programs will be successful only if they are planned to work together with programs to help people start businesses, plan their families' futures, and improve their children's health. This is not an easy task, but hundreds of students graduating from Bangladesh's universities are committed to their country's future. This generation of "true Bangladeshis" will bring new energy to the work of educating Bangladesh's rural citizens.

8. Sports and Games Outdoors

Although Bangladeshi children must work and study very hard, they also love to play. Schoolchildren play cricket, soccer, and volleyball, and participate in P.T. (physical training) as part of every school day. In P.T., they exercise, play organized games, and run relay races. Village children make their own fun in the countryside around them.

Because Bangladesh has so many streams and rivers, village children grow up playing in the water. Most learn to swim at an early age. Boat races and water polo are more common than other games during the hot season, and older children may practice for the community races that are part of many festivals. Children also enjoy riding inner tubes down the rivers, but they need to watch out for the dangerous snakes that often live in the water.

The most popular sport in Bangladeshi cities is soccer, which everyone calls football. Dhaka Stadium is a popular place to cheer local and regional teams. A government institute, the *Bangladesh Krira Shikka Protishthan*, trains promising players, maintains sports standards, and awards scholarships for its athletes to attend training seminars in other countries.

Children enjoy a playground in Dhaka.

Boat races, such as this one, are common on Bangladesh's many waterways.

Bangladesh in the World of Sports

Bangladesh's first chance to participate in the Olympic Games came in the summer of 1984. The nation's only representative was Saidur Rahman Dawn, a 21-year-old psychology student from Rajshahi Division. Dawn was called the "Gang of One from Bangladesh." Although he did not place in his two events, the 100- and 200-meter sprints, his presence at the Olympics in Los Angeles was a matter of honor and pride for his family, his nation, and the several thousand Bangla-

The opening ceremony of the South Asia Federation Games, held in Dhaka in 1985.

deshis living in the United States. He was a lone, proud figure carrying the green and red Bangladeshi flag into the opening ceremonies between the huge groups from Australia and China.

The South Asia Federation Games were held in Dhaka in 1985. In these games, teams from many Asian countries join in Olympic-style competition. One of the games is cricket, a popular sport throughout Bangladesh. Cricket is much like baseball in the United States.

It is a team sport played with a bat and ball, and it has innings. However, the bat is long and flat, and the players wear padded leggings and safari-style hats.

Cricket is played on a rectangular field. On each end are "wickets" made of three poles, with little sticks called "bails" lying across the top. The batsman stands at one end of the field, and the pitcher (called a "bowler") stands at the other. The bowler tries to knock the bails off the wickets, and the batsman tries to hit the ball before that happens. When the ball is hit, the batsman and one teammate run back and forth between the wickets to score runs, while the bowler continues to try to knock off the bails. If the bowler knocks a bail off the wickets, the batsman is out. Cricket is a common afterschool activity. Usually, someone in the neighborhood will have a bat and ball to share!

Kabaddi and *Gul Tara*

Soccer, cricket, and tennis were brought to Bengal during British rule. Another very popular game in Bangladesh started in India when Bangladesh was still an Indian state. *Kabaddi* is a unique team sport because it requires no equipment. It is also the only field game in the world with categories for age and weight.

A kabaddi team has twelve players, but only seven play at one time. A match consists of twenty-minute halves for men or fifteen-minute halves for women and children, with a five-minute break in between halves. Kabaddi is actually a sophisticated form of tag.

Each kabaddi team has its own court, which is divided in the middle by a "baulk" line. One side sends a "raider" into the opponent's court. The opponents are called "antis" (anti-raiders). Before crossing the center line, the raider must begin to say *"kabaddi, kabaddi, kabaddi,"* over and over again, without taking a breath. The raider must say it loudly and clearly so that the referees can hear. This is called the "cant." The raider tries to touch as many of the antis as possible before going back to his or her own court. The raider must cross the antis' baulk line at least once, and can touch opponents with any part of the body. If the raider succeeds in crossing the baulk line, touching one or more antis, and returning to his or her court without losing the cant (running out of breath and not saying "kabaddi"), all the antis that he or she touched are out, or "dead."

However, if the raider loses the cant or is captured by the antis, he or she is out. If the raider returns without touching anyone and without losing the cant, neither side loses a player. The side with the most "living" players at the end of the game wins. This game is also called *ha-do-do* in Bangladesh, and it is very popular with children and adults alike.

Gul tara, which means "throwing to the stars," is another Indian game that many Bangladeshis enjoy. One player throws a ball high up in the air, and all the others rush to catch it. The player who catches the ball throws it up again. If no one catches it, all the players scatter except the one who threw the ball. This player must pick the ball up and try to tag another player with it. The player who is tagged becomes the "horse," and must carry the first player on his or her back while that player again throws the ball "to the stars." The player who catches the ball gets to change places with the rider. If the horse catches the ball, he or she changes places with the rider. If no one catches it, the horse gets the ball and tries to tag someone—and then the game starts again.

Festival Games

Festivals are a time when Bangladeshis can have informal cricket matches and play games like *lukuchuri* (hide-and-seek), *kanamachi* (blindman's bluff), jump rope, and *satchara*. To play satchara, children put seven tiles upright on a wall or a box, and divide into two teams. The first team tries to knock the tiles down with a soft ball, while the second team scurries to replace them. If the second team can successfully replace all the tiles without being tagged by the ball, they win. A

Young Bangladeshi men display their skill at lathi khela, *a type of martial art.*

person who is hit by the ball is out of the game. If the first team can knock down all the tiles or tag all of the second team's players within seven tries, they win.

At a festival in Bangladesh, there is plenty of music, dancing, drama, food, and games. There are even rides, such as a hand-turned ferris wheel or a ride in the *howdah* (seat) on top of a huge elephant. Older boys like to practice a martial art called *lathi khela*, or stick-fighting. Some boys become skilled enough with the lathi khela moves to demonstrate them for festival audiences.

A game for smaller children, usually girls, is called "nurse and child." The "nurse" sits on the ground, while the "child" sits on her lap, facing outward with legs extended. The nurse blindfolds the child's eyes with her hands, and, one by one, the other players step over the child's legs. The child must guess who is stepping over her legs. If the child guesses correctly, she gets to be the nurse, the player who was caught becomes the child, and the nurse joins the group.

Whether they are at festivals or at home, Bangladeshi children enjoy the games and sports they play. Many of these games are as much a part of their heritage as the stories they hear from their grandparents and the folk dances they learn from their parents. It is a heritage that Bangladeshis will take with them as their country grows.

9. *Bangladeshis Share Their Heritage*

Most of Bangladesh's more than 100 million people could not imagine traveling outside their country, much less going to the United States. Yet, because the world's people are moving closer through television, international business, and government programs, the Bangladeshi and American people are beginning to share experiences and are getting to know one another better.

Opportunities for Students

Upper-class Bangladeshis sometimes visit the United States. Many of these families also want to send their college-age children to U.S. universities since they believe that their sons and daughters may get better jobs as a result of an American education.

Being in the United States is a mixed blessing for Bangladeshi students. Leaving their families behind is often painful and difficult. The close-knit Bangladeshi family provides a sense of belonging and a deeply rooted feeling of security. The rich Bengali culture is also part of every Bangladeshi's life. It can be quite a shock for them to come to the United States, which is completely different from Bangladesh in many respects.

In the United States, the food, clothing, language, climate, family relations, customs, manners, and pace of everyday life can be overwhelming to a newly arrived Bangladeshi. Some adjust rapidly and enjoy the differences. As one Bangladeshi student said, "America is a good place to find oneself because of the personal freedom available here."

Respected Immigrants

Since 1974, more than six thousand people from Bangladesh have moved to the United States. Several thousand more come to visit each year. Most have settled on the East and West Coasts of the United States, in areas where other Asian and Indian people live. Most Bangladeshis who immigrate to the United States are highly educated and skilled. Many are leaders in large corporations or professors at universities. Some work in or own import, travel, or retail businesses. They are looking for opportunities to better their lives in a new country.

A United States citizen who is a native of Bangladesh is one of America's leading structural engineers. Fazlur Rahman Khan was born and educated in Dhaka. He and a co-worker invented several new ways to construct extremely tall buildings. He designed the tubular frame, a system of strong, but light, support structures that makes it possible to build very tall buildings which can withstand the force of high winds. These inventions led Khan and a co-worker, Bruce Graham, to design the 1,454-foot (443-meter) tall Sears Tower in Chicago, the tallest building in the world.

Preserving Bangladeshi Culture

Bangladeshi parents in the United States want their children to find an identity which combines the best of both the American and Bengali cultures. The parents feel that it is important to teach Bengali values, language, and history to their children from an early age. Then, as the children grow up American, they will not forget the richness of their heritage.

Bangladeshi couples and families in the United States usually try to maintain their culture while they adapt to the American way of life. "Living with one foot in each culture can be a difficult thing," says Sartaz Aziz, a college professor in Massachusetts. "It requires constant choices....I hope my child will be able to incorporate the best of Bengali culture and the best of American attitudes into a single life. I know that is hard, but isn't that what America is all about?"

Maintaining their culture can be difficult because the Bangladeshi population in the United States is so small. Bangladeshi immigrant children have little

Sartaz Aziz, a Bangladeshi college professor now living in the United States.

opportunity to play with one another, and there is little community support as compared with other ethnic groups in the United States. However, organizations have been founded to help Bangladeshis find one another and to sponsor religious and cultural festivals.

The Bangladesh Association has its center in Cambridge, Massachusetts. This association brings together Bangladeshis from all over the East Coast. On the Bengali New Year they host a Bengali feast and celebration which includes dance, drama, and speeches by Bangladeshis in the area. One of the Association's newest

Bangladeshi-American children present a program at a Bengali celebration sponsored by the Bangladesh Assocation.

projects is a school, called *Ankoor* ("sprout" or "embryo"). In this school, which is housed in a classroom at the Massachusetts Institute of Technology, Bangladeshi children are taught about their cultural heritage and their parents' birthplace. They learn the Bengali language and create programs about Bengali culture to present at the annual festivals.

One of the Ankoor's productions was a drama based on a cyclone that struck the coastal town of Urirachar in 1984. By staging this drama about rural life in Bangladesh, the children learned about their parents' homeland, and they shared their culture with Americans. This positive identification with Bangladesh is an important part of their education.

Changing Impressions

Many Americans first learned about Bangladesh during the 1971 war of liberation, when war, floods, and famine made conditions in the country very bad. At that time, rock singer George Harrison organized a big concert in New York City to raise funds to help victims of the disasters that nearly destroyed Bangladesh. For a long time, pictures of those terrible conditions were many Americans' only impression of Bangladesh.

Bangladesh is one of the poorest countries in the world, but conditions are slowly changing. The people of Bangladesh feel that they are the guardians of ancient treasures and the pioneers of a new country. Like Americans, they prize the freedom that cost them so much. The joyous cry of *"Jai Bangla!"* can still be heard in Bangladesh and from the Bangladeshi people who are beginning to share their culture with the United States and the world.

Appendix

Bangladeshi Embassies and Consulates in the United States and Canada

The Bangladeshi consulates in the United States and Canada offer assistance and information about all aspects of Bangladeshi life. For information and resource materials about Bangladesh, contact the embassy or consulate nearest you.

U.S. Consulates and Embassy

Los Angeles, California
   Honorary Consulate General of Bangladesh
   10981 Bellagio Road
   Los Angeles, California 90024
   Phone (213) 532-2963

New York, New York
   Consulate General of Bangladesh
   821 United Nations Plaza
   New York, New York 10017
   Phone (212) 867-3434

Washington, D.C.
   Embassy of Bangladesh
   2201 Wisconsin Avenue, Northwest
   Washington, D.C. 20007
   Phone (202) 342-8376

Canadian Embassy

Ottawa, Ontario
   Embassy of Bangladesh
   85 Range Road, Suite 402
   Ottawa, Ontario K1N 8J6
   Phone (613) 236-0138

Glossary

Akika (ah·KEE·kuh)—the Muslim ceremony in which a baby is given his or her "good" name

Allah (AH·luh)—the Muslim name for God

alu (AH·loo)—potato

amar (ah·MAHR)—my, mine

ankoor (UHN·koor)—sprout or embryo; also the name for a school for Bangladeshi children in the United States

Ashura (ah·SHOOR·uh)—a Muslim holiday celebrated on the first ten days of the month of *Maharram*

atman (AHT·muhn)—the Hindu word for "soul"

Baishakh (by·SHAHK)—a month in the Bengali calendar

Baishakhi Purnima (by·SHAHK·ee poor·NEE·mah)—a Buddhist holiday celebrating the birth of Buddha

Banglabandhu (buhng·luh·BUHN·dhoo)—a friend of the Bengalis; *bandhu* means "friend"

Bangladesh (buhng·luh·DEHSH)—land of the Bengalis; *desh* means "land or country"

Bangladeshi (buhng·luh·DEHSH·ee)—someone born in Bangladesh

bel (bayl)—jackfruit

bharta (BHAHR·tuh)—spicy mashed potatoes

bhikhu (BHEE·koo)—a Buddhist priest

biryani (beer·YAH·nee)—any dish made with meat and rice mixed together

boti (BOH·tee)—a special knife used to cut vegetables

burfi (BUR·fee)—a dessert made from milk

burkha (BUR·kah)—a cloth used to cover a woman from her head all the way to the ground, with a screen across the eyes to see out

chappati (chuh·PAH·tee)—round, flat bread

charpoy (CHAHR·poy)—a bed made from rope

dal (dahl)—spicy cooked lentils

dav (dahb)—green coconut

dhoti (DHOH·tee)—a white cloth worn like loose-fitting pants by Hindu men

Diwali (dee·WAH·lee)—the Hindu festival of lights; also called *Diipavali*

Durga Puja (DOOR·gah POO·jah)—a Hindu festival to celebrate the goddess Kali

gandharaj (guhn·duh·RAHJ)—gardenia; *gandha* means "scent," *raj* means "king"

gul tara (gool TAH·ruh)—a children's game; *gul tara* means "throwing to the stars"

ha-do-do (hah·doh·DOH)—another name for the game *kabaddi*

Hathi Khori (HAH·tee KHOH·ree)—the Muslim ceremony to introduce a child to education by writing the alphabet; *hathi* means "hand," *khori* means "chalk"

hilsa (HEEL·suh)—a fish found in Bangladesh's rivers

hing (hihng)—a spice used in place of garlic; also called *asafoetida*

Holi (HOH·lee)—a Hindu festival celebrating the legend of Krishna

Id (eed)—a Muslim holy day

Id-ul-Azha (eed·uhl·AHJ·uh)—a Muslim holiday in memory of the story of Abraham

Id-ul-Fitr (eed·uhl·FEET)—a Muslim holiday that starts on the new moon after *Ramadan*

jai (joy)—victory

Jai Bangla (joy BUHNG·luh)—victory to the Bengalis; a phrase used during the 1971 war for independence

jamdani (jahm·DAH·nee)—Bangladeshi silk woven for *sari*s and shawls

jatra (JUH·truh)—a folk opera combining music, dance, poetry, and drama

kabaddi (kuh·BAH·dee)—a team sport invented in India

kamiz (kuh·MEEZ)—a long, fitted tunic worn over a *salwar*

kanamachi (kahn·uh·MAH·chee)—a children's game like blindman's bluff

kantha (KAHN·tah)—a quilt or piece of embroidery

khela (KHEH·lah)—to play a game

Koran (kohr·AHN)—the Muslim holy book

lathi (LAH·tee)—a long bamboo stick used in *lathi khela*; also used by the police as a weapon

lathi khela (LAH·tee KHEH·lah)—stick-fighting, a type of martial arts

luchi (LOO·chee)—fried bread

lukuchuri (loo·koo·CHUR·ee)—a children's game like hide-and-seek

lungi (LUHN·gee)—a cloth worn tucked at the waist by men and boys

Mahabharata (mah·hah·BHAHR·uh·tuh)—a very long poem in the Hindu religion

maharaja (mah·hah·RAH·juh)—king

Maharram (muh·huh·RAHM)—the first month of the Muslim calendar

Manipuri (moh·nee·PUR·ee)—a classical dance

masala (MUH·shuhl·uh)—ground spices; also a paste made of ground spices

mosque (mahsk)—a Muslim place of worship

moulvi (MOHL·vee)—a Muslim priest

mul-mul (MOOL·mool)—a type of cloth called muslin

muri (MUR·ee)—puffed rice

pandal (PUHN·duhl)—a big, gaily decorated tent

purdah (PUR·dah)—the Muslim custom in which women are required to keep their faces covered in front of men

Ramadan (RUHM·uh·duhn)—the Muslim month of fasting

Ramayana (ruhm·EYE·uh·nuh)—an important story in the Hindu religion

rangoli (ruhng·OH·lee)—a picture created on the ground with colored powders or flower petals

salwar (SHAHL·wahr)—pants which are gathered at the waist and the ankles, worn by girls and by some Muslim women

sari (SAH·ree)—a long piece of cloth which is wound around the body and folded and tucked in a particular way, worn by most women in Bangladesh; a *sari* is worn over a tight-fitting cotton blouse and petticoat

satchara (shaht·CHAH·ruh)—a children's game; *satchara* means "seven times"

shiil nora (sheel NOH·rah)—a smooth black rock used to grind spices

shingara (shihng·AHR·ah)—a vegetable- or meat-stuffed pastry

sika (SEE·kah)—a long braid of jute, knotted artistically and used to hang pots from ceiling rafters

sitar (see·TAHR)—a stringed instrument

suji (SHOOH·jee)—semolina or cream of wheat

sura (SUR·ah)—a Muslim prayer

tabla (TUH·bluh)—a small drum

taka (TAH·kah)—the Bangladeshi unit of money

thakur ghar (TUH·koor ghohr)—a family shrine

vyamer chata (bang·ayr CHUH·tuh)—a mushroom; *vyamer* means "frog's," *chata* means "umbrella"

Zilhaj (jeel·HAHJ)—a month in the Muslim calendar

Selected Bibliography

Baxter, Craig. *Bangladesh: A New Nation in an Old Setting.* Boulder, Colorado: Westview Press, 1984.

Chen, Martha Alter. *A Quiet Revolution: Women in Transition in Rural Bangladesh.* Cambridge, Massachusetts: Schenkman, 1983.

Franda, Marcus. *Bangladesh, the First Decade.* New Delhi, India: South Asian Publishers, 1982.

Kabir, Humayun. *Green and Gold: Stories and Poems from Bengal.* Norfolk, Connecticut: New Directions, 1958.

Karim, Abul Nazmul. *The Dynamics of Bangladesh Society.* New Delhi, India: Vikas, 1980.

Mascarenhas, Anthony. *Bangladesh: A Legacy of Blood.* London: Hodder and Stoughton, 1986.

Mukherjee, Prabhat Kumar. *Life of Tagore.* Thompson, Connecticut: Inter Culture Associates, 1975.

O'Donnell, Charles Peter. *Bangladesh: Biography of a Muslim Nation.* Boulder, Colorado: Westview Press, 1984.

Index

About the Author

Vimala McClure has traveled to India and Bangladesh many times since 1973. "My Bengali friends are like family to me," she says. "The Bengali culture has so much to share with other cultures in the world. I am delighted to have the opportunity to write about it for American children."

Mrs. McClure is a writer and an infant parenting educator. She has written several books and many magazine articles for parents with new babies. She lives in the Ozark mountains of southern Missouri with her husband and three children.